FINDING AGAPE

Perfectly loved

By

NINA LEIGH FORD

Contents

Dedication

All glory to God.

This book is dedicated to my grandchildren, Alyssa Taylon, Carmen Elizabeth, Brilee Leann, Nevaeh Adalynn and Dakota Shane. May your lives bring glory to the Lord. You deserve a world where there is no pain or sorrow.

Introduction

God's word in 2 Corinthians 10:3-5 say:

For though we walk in the flesh, we are not waging war according to the flesh. For the weapons of our warfare are not of the flesh but have divine power to destroy strongholds. We destroy arguments every lofty opinion raised against the knowledge of God, and take every thought captive to obey Christ.

Children are without knowledge until their parents teach them the ways they grow into. When learning from a parent who suffers from drug addictions, mental illness, generational curses, and demons that haunt their soul, the endless torture of one's childhood often leads their children down a path of destruction, pain, and suffering into adulthood.

But God, so loving, and full of kindness rescues from darkness. This is my truth and testimony.

Chapter 1
In The Beginning

My father was raised by an alcoholic father and a mother who physically and sexually abused him, just as their parents had done to them. My mother's father was sexually abusive to his five daughters. My mother's mother, on the other hand, was a sweet and kind Pentecostal woman. In the 1950s, when my parents were born, people simply didn't talk about what went on behind closed doors. They were ashamed, fearing that if anyone found out, their reputations would be tarnished in the public eye.

My parents married at the age of 16. They came from humble beginnings but soon started a family. My sister was born in the spring of 1970, and I was born in the winter of '71, by which time they had moved to a different state. My brother came in the spring of '74. Seventeen years later, in the summer of '89, my youngest brother was born.

My very first memory from my childhood is from December of 1975, the day before my fifth birthday. I was so excited because Maw Maw and Paw Paw had come to the garage apartment where my parents had just finished packing to move us to a house across town. They brought me a beautiful, fluffy, lace-trimmed orange dress for my birthday. I hugged and thanked Maw Maw, then Mom sent me downstairs to thank Paw Paw, who was outside smoking a cigarette in the driveway.

He motioned for me to climb onto his lap. I climbed up and hugged his neck, when I suddenly felt him put his hand between my legs and move his fingers to rub my vagina. I was very uncomfortable, so I quickly hopped down and ran back upstairs. I grabbed my dress, and my dad told me to hang it up in my empty closet. Thinking nothing of it, I did as I was told.

When it was time to leave, I started back upstairs to get the dress, but my dad met me halfway and told me to go to the car. When I said I wanted my dress, he spanked me. As we pulled away, I cried, watching through the back window as we left without it.

After we settled into the new house, both Mom and Dad got jobs. Most days, we were left with my older sister, who was only six at the time; bossy and mean most of the time. We began riding the church bus that came through our neighborhood, and by the time I turned six, we had been going for a while.

Dad had either lost his job or got home before Mom, giving him plenty of time to torment us and do ungodly things before she returned. When he wasn't raping me, he forced us to read books and write reports. We were beaten severely if we didn't finish on time. He made us copy the Bible word for word until our fingertips bled.

Sometimes, I could hear screams coming from the upstairs bedroom. Sometimes I knew which child it was, other times, we weren't sure who his victim would be next.

Realizing now, my dad was a serial child predator. Back then, it felt normal, we dared not say anything, afraid we'd be the next to face his wrath. I must have been his favorite target, as I was most often at the receiving end of his pain. I was so terrified of him that I froze whenever he called my name, powerless to escape whatever came next.

Over time, I became accustomed to the pain, confusing it with love because he always said he loved me while inflicting it. I didn't realize until much later that, for most of my life, if something didn't hurt, it didn't feel like love to me and that it would lead me down a path Satan himself had a hand in.

Chapter 2

The Age Of Unending Pain

I never saw him take my brother or sister upstairs, but that's where my hell began. At the age of five, my dad sent the other kids to play outside and locked the door. He went upstairs, drew a bath, then came back down and told me to go upstairs and get into the tub. You never questioned my dad, or you risked facing his wrath.

I undressed and got into the bath, hurriedly washing and drying myself before reaching for my clothes. He said, "NO! Come over here."

When he told me to, I did as I was told and made my way to the bed where he was sitting. He grabbed my arm, led me to the side of the bed, then lifted me by the shoulders and threw me onto it. He grabbed my legs pulling me to him and spread my legs. I didn't understand what was happening till he grabbed at his belt and started taking it off. He hastily unbuttoned his pants, unzipping and letting them fall to the floor.

The first few times this happened, he just rubbed his penis on my vagina and ejaculated on me. Most of the times, there was no pain involved. But soon, that all changed. As if beating me with belts, extension cords or making me pick switches to be beat with, throwing shoes or horseshoes wasn't enough, he changed his routine.

One day, after the bath and him discarding his clothes, he pulled me to him and instead of the usual, using his full force, he penetrated me. The pain was so much that I started screaming. My father grabbed a pillow and pushed it in my face long enough for me to pass out. God must have allowed me to pass out, because everything went dark. I don't remember the pain of the rape on that day, only waking up later. That blackout, I believe, was God's way of protecting me from the unbearable pain of that moment. I realize today that it was God showing me mercy from the countless times of this happening. God must have sent his angels to surround me.

After I realized that "upstairs" meant pain, I began to fight him every time he tried to take me there. That's when he would force me upstairs into the tub, holding me under the water until I stopped moving. I couldn't breathe but my eyes could still see him. He removed me from the tub and gave me CPR. Before I could finish coughing up the water, he threw me on the bed again. As I just laid there, no movement, no sound, he continued to rape and sodomize me.

After a while, I stopped fighting him. I just didn't have any strength left. He had broken me completely.

We still went to church regularly, and that's where I first found Jesus, around the age of six or seven. My home life was unbearable. One Sunday, the preacher said, "Would you like a Father who will always be there for you, who is kind, and who loves you unconditionally?"

I remember raising my hand, desperate to know that kind of love; to have a Father I could go home to, instead of the one waiting for me. They led me and a few others to a small room where we prayed for Jesus to come into our hearts.

On the ride back, when the church bus pulled into my neighborhood, I refused to get off. I clung to the seat, crying and screaming that I was supposed to go home to Jesus' house, not mine. My sister and the driver had to pry me away. In that moment, I felt trapped, condemned to a life of torment. My hell wasn't over; it had only just begun, here on earth.

As time went on, Dad found new ways to torture us; pulling our loose teeth with channel locks, making us kneel on raw rice on the wooden kitchen floor while he watched from his chair in the living room, or bringing dogs home for us to love, only to take them away months later. He would even drive us across town while drunk and leave us to find our own way home.

On the days another child or teen was in the house, I was grateful for the freedom to play outside and run through the neighborhood. Sometimes we got into trouble, doing mischievous things, destroying abandoned houses, setting mailboxes on fire, or even breaking into a neighbor's back door to grab candy off the kitchen counter. My brother and I certainly paid dearly for that one. We were given hundred lashes bare-bottom with his leather belt. Dad made us count each lick out loud.

We couldn't sit for a week or more. Our skin split open, and the wounds bled through our clothes, weeping for weeks. The school saw the pain we were in but did nothing to help. It seemed no one ever had the courage to say anything to my parents.

Everyone around that could help failed us daily. Could they not see the bruises or us acting out?

Chapter 3

Can't Remember Her Name

Dad was deliberate with his cruelty. As time went on, when I reached the age of twelve, a new family moved into the house across the street, a mother and her two daughters, one around eight and the other three. They were of color. The mother had a 16-year-old brother who was there quite often. I quickly made it known that I was interested in him, and he was equally smitten with me.

We started spending a lot of time together. We would usually engage in prolong conversations, until one day he and I were alone in the shed. Before I knew it, the doors were closed and we were all over each other, I kissing him, and him kissing me. It was so obvious that we wanted each other.

Out of nowhere, I heard my dad calling for me, and I was shaken to my core. I think he saw us go into the shed together from the window. Terrified, I asked the boy, the young man, to please stay inside until I got home and shut the door behind me. I knew he had seen us when he asked, "Who were you in the shed with?"

But before I could even answer, he dragged me upstairs and beat me so hard I could barely breathe. He then continued to rape, like he would, always.

Soon, around 1984, Dad had us start inviting the girls to go to the park with us. We'd play baseball, and often football, before heading out for ice cream. Their mom trusted my dad and let them go with us, just the three of us, without question.

A few months after the meeting in the shed, the youngest girl disappeared from her yard while we were at school. I can't even remember her name now....

That day, the local police combed the streets, searching for her. They came to our house, but Dad wasn't home, and Mom was at work. They left their card for Mom to call them back.

The police put out a description of a suspect, but the girl wasn't found until months later, when a fisherman spotted her body in a canal in a neighboring state. Her autopsy stated that she had drowned, but by the time they found her, she was so decomposed that it was all they could determine about what happened to that poor baby girl.

It's funny how soon after, Mom and Dad separated, then divorced. Coincidence? I think not. Mom and us kids moved into an apartment where we were left to get ourselves to school and prepare dinner for when Mom came home from work. We spent the best Christmases there, and all our birthdays were filled with happiness. We even had a few friends over to celebrate. Those were the best times of my life. We were allowed to go to the pool almost anytime, and even enjoyed the hot tub on the complex grounds.

But good things rarely last. Suddenly, we were forced to move back to the family home, and all those painful memories came flooding back. I no longer enjoyed life, and suicide increasingly became part of my thought pattern.

When Dad started coming around again, I could tell his drinking had gotten worse. He reeked of alcohol all day, every day. When Mom let him move back in, I couldn't take it anymore. I ran away.

I rode my bike to the big bridge, planning to jump, when a stranger approached and, just close enough, grabbed me. That kind man saved my life that day. I believe God must have sent him. Angels can look like city workers.

I never got the chance to thank him. He loaded my bike and took me to the police station, where they used anatomically correct dolls to take my statement, and I was placed into foster care. From there, I was sent to live with an aunt because of drug use in the foster home, specifically, by the foster mom's daughter.

I finished eighth grade there but was sent back home. I wished to return to my aunt's, but I couldn't convince my parents to send me. I felt as though God had abandoned me yet again. I didn't want to live anymore and often thought about how I could end it all.

Chapter 4

The Injustice

I remember sitting outside the courtroom, waiting to testify against my Dad. But I was never called in. I had hoped Mom would finally speak up about the time she caught him in the house with me, naked, with the door locked. I remembered peering around the corner of the hall, and when she saw me, she beat me across my back and told me not to walk around the house naked. Like I had a choice, or as if I had somehow been deliberately enticing my dad.

I never understood why I was blamed for things he was doing to me. *Wasn't I the victim? I was being raped that day, and yet, she blamed me. She could have protected me but chose not to.*

He walked out free that day. I wasn't protected, not once again. The church we had been attending since we were kids became part of our lives again after the trial, Mom and Dad joined after. We were in AWANA for a while, but then Mom and Dad separated again. I think he was in rehab at the time.

That's when I met Duck. I was a fourteen-year-old freshman in high school, and he was a sixteen-year-old junior, best friends with my sister's boyfriend. By that time, Dad had left Mom for someone he met in rehab.

Duck and I became inseparable. Nothing could tear us apart. I snuck out of the house many nights with my sister to meet up with him and his friend, and we'd cruise the town together, smoking weed and having sex. Unprotected.

Duck would help my mom with groceries and often stay to eat. We didn't want to be apart from each other. I was so in love with him.

This went on for two years, until Dad came back into the home and threatened to put him in jail for statutory rape, since he had just turned eighteen and I was still only sixteen. Dad always seemed determined to make sure I never had any happiness or joy. I think he was just jealous because he could not have sex with me anymore.

Letting him go broke me once again. He was the only person who had never hurt me, and I couldn't bear the thought of him going to jail, so I ended the relationship. For his sake.

Our family became more involved with the church, and my parents became friends with several members. Mom and Dad were remarried in that church. The mask my Dad wore was so convincing.

I wanted to be baptized on the day I was to dedicate my life to God. As I stood in the baptismal waters, the preacher announced that my Dad would be baptized with me. I was in disbelief. My worst fear had somehow come true. *What do you mean?* I had thought. The man who had drowned me in the tub so many times as a child, now in the water with me? The preacher proceeded with both baptisms, and the congregation applauded as I stood there, terrified that he would drown me again.

Why couldn't anyone see through his charade? Why was the woman who raised me still enabling this monster? My faith in God and in my mom to protect me flew out the door that day. I blamed God for everything that had happened to me up until then. I wanted to disappear. I lost the faith I once had in God.

My Mother wanted another baby, so she took steps to have her IUD removed and soon became pregnant with my baby brother. Around that time, my Dad attempted suicide by drinking Ortho, which landed him in the ICU for a long while. My sister moved out, and I stayed with her as she was now married and pregnant. Soon after, my baby brother was born.

By this time, I had met a guy, started dating him, and was soon engaged myself. Dad recovered from the suicide attempt, but when my baby brother was almost one, Mother called us all together for a family meeting. Since we were all living our own lives, we met at the family home. She said there was something she needed to discuss with all of us, something that couldn't be done over the phone.

When we arrived, Mom and Dad were waiting for us. We had a long talk before Dad announced he would be turning himself in for the kidnapping of the little four-year-old girl that disappeared when we were children. I asked him if he had killed her and he said no.

I couldn't forget what the news had reported, and knowing what he had done to me; the rapes, the drownings, the beatings, I knew he was lying. There were many children I saw Dad bring upstairs in those early years. Looking back now, I understand he was a serial rapist.

Mother had known for four years about the kidnapping and didn't turn him in, all because of her selfish desire to have another child to love, knowing Dad would be going to prison for a long time.

He went to trial and was sentenced to twenty-five years in prison. All glory to God, my baby brother would never have to endure what us older kids went through. His 25-year sentence eventually became a life sentence. He is still incarcerated to this day.

Chapter 5

Damaged Goods

When Steve and I met, I was still in school and working two jobs. He was so handsome, and every girl wanted him, but I managed to get him. The girls were so jealous at church and school. If they had only seen my future, they would have warned me to stay far away from him, for Satan himself lived deep inside him. We were married at the courthouse in 1990.

I remember Dad telling him that I was 'damaged goods' and that if I ever gave my husband any trouble or didn't listen, he should just beat me until I did.

The first time Steve hit me, it was completely unexpected. He had been drinking and told me to get him a beer. When I said I needed to use the bathroom first, I was met with a violent, open-handed slap to the face. He quickly gained the upper hand with physical force, and with my upbringing, I felt I had no choice but to submit, like an obedient dog.

We soon moved in with Steve's mother and stepdad, and his sister lived there as well. She didn't like me at all and treated me as if I wasn't good enough for Steve. I became pregnant with my oldest son and gave birth to him in the summer of 1991. I was so blessed to be a mom. His bright brown eyes lit up when I held him, and I finally felt the unconditional love I had always longed for. He became the love I never had before, and my son made my life worth living.

Soon, we bought a house far from town, in the country. It was a three-bedroom, one-bath house on an acre of land in the woods, secluded from family and society. Steve would have bonfires constantly, and I was obedient to his every want and need. But his drinking became uncontrollable, as did the abuse. He even used my toddler son to hurt me by not letting me hold him or tend to him when he cried or needed me.

Finally, I found the courage to leave him and moved in with my mother. I had some freedom to go out with a female relative and visit other families' houses, where I met James. He looked like an angel, as if God Himself had sent him. We were together just one night, but we produced a daughter. James was from Louisiana and went back home. We lost touch, as there were no cell phones back then.

During this time, I was still allowing Steve to visit his son. He convinced me that he had changed, that he would never hit me again, so we reunited. I had to tell him I was pregnant, and he seemed accepting of it. We moved back to the house with him.

Chapter 6

Broken beyond repair

The downward spiral began soon after. Apparently, being pregnant with another man's baby was a problem, and I quickly learned just how much. Some days, things were fine, but then his family would get to him, and the beatings became worse. He started drinking again, and the friends he had met during our separation would join him at his bonfires. My role became to serve them beer whenever they needed it.

The more he drank, the meaner he became. There were days when he would force me to drink, and when I tried to refuse, he would knock me out cold and leave me lying on the ground, surrounded by ants. His friends never stepped up to defend me. I had lost all hope in men, and God felt like a distant thought.

As my belly grew, so did the cruelty he showed me. It became unbearable. One day, I decided to plan, and to leave. My plan was to execute it after the baby was born.

But it was on the day I finally made up my mind to leave that he had his friends over again and beat me so badly that I collapsed on the kitchen floor, crying and unable to move. I urinated myself, too weak to get up, and the pool of urine quickly became a pool of blood. Despite this, he refused to take me to the hospital, wanting me to lose the baby.

In a state of complete surrender, I lay there for two days, nine months pregnant, with no help.

Two weeks later, my baby girl was delivered by C-section. As soon as she was born, everyone gathered to welcome her into the world, and my heart was overwhelmed with love and joy. She was the most beautiful little angel I had ever seen. She looked just like my baby pictures, with long, coal-black hair. My mother was in the surgery room with me, as my husband refused to be there since she wasn't his child. I think the only reason he even held her was because his mother said she looked just like him, which made him believe she was his. He allowed me to give her his last name.

Once I recovered from surgery, things took a turn for the worse. He needed money for beer and weed, so he made me start working at a strip club in the next city. That place became, ironically, my only refuge, a small pocket of peace and solitude away from the abuse, but it was also a downward spiral for my future. The only way I could save myself was by secretly hiding money and keeping my earnings from him.

But before I could even think about moving away, something unexpected happened. One night, after he and his friends had been drinking, his sister's boyfriend showed up late at the house. A fight broke out when his friends came inside while my husband was passed out, and they tried to rape me. Luckily, he caught them at the back door and beat them up. I called the police, and they arrested my husband, but by the time they arrived, his friends had scattered.

While Steve was in jail, his sister's boyfriend came to the house and raped me. I had never been so terrified of telling Steve when he got home the next morning, but somehow, I managed to keep things calm. He told me he couldn't live there anymore and sold the house for a two-bedroom trailer and three cars. We moved across town, closer to society, but he continued the beatings.

One day, I went to get coffee from a neighbor, and he thought I was sleeping with the man. When I told him I wasn't, he didn't believe me. In a fit of rage, he held me down on the bed, shoved a sawed-off shotgun in my mouth, and pulled the trigger. That's when I knew

God had other plans for me. The gun jammed, and I kicked him off of me, running out the back door. I had to leave my children behind to escape, fearing he would kill me.

I called the police and my mother. The police let him keep the kids, though they didn't believe me for some reason. I had to go with my mom, with no money, no clothes, and without my children.

I felt like I had lost my soul. Satan's grip on me deepened that day. My future seemed non-existent. I had stopped caring about everything.

Chapter 7
Spiraling

I became promiscuous, sleeping with whoever I chose, telling myself, "What's the flavor of the day?" I stayed with a much younger man for a while. He was 19, and I was 25. I kept dancing at the clubs, stacking a little cash, living a life that was far from what I ever imagined. But then, God revealed a secret that my mother had been keeping from me.

One day, I went to visit her, and to my shock, I found her with my two children, whom I hadn't seen in over a year. She hadn't even bothered to tell me they were there. What kind of mother doesn't tell her daughter that her children are with her? I was livid, heartbroken, and angry at the nerve of her. That day, I took custody of my children, vowing to never let them go again.

My life immediately shifted back to being about the kids. I stopped dancing and started working a legitimate job. I became a mother to my children once more, determined to give them the love and care they deserved.

Six months after that day, the boy I had been staying with body-slammed me on the beach during spring break, and I had no choice but to move back in with my mom. A few years went by before I met another young guy, 19, staying the summer with his dad across the street from my mother's. I should have known better, but with my history, my sexual needs often took priority. I always jumped in blindly, not giving much thought to the men I'd been with.

After about three months, I found myself pregnant again. He seemed excited, hoping for a little girl. I wasn't quite ready for another child, but here I was again. All I could do was laugh at my situation. He found a job, and eventually, we moved into a place in the same neighborhood as Mom. When I was about eight months pregnant, he moved us across the state to Dallas, where his mom and stepdad were living with his two brothers. We stayed in the living room of their small two-bedroom apartment until I gave birth to his son. The baby looked just like his dad, but with blonde hair and the most beautiful blue eyes. I was completely in love with my baby boy.

We moved into our own apartment in the same complex, and things seemed to be going as well as they could. He worked regularly, and I stayed home with the kids. He wasn't the type to put his hands on me or drink excessively. Looking back, I can't believe I didn't see it, how everything seemed too good to be true.

Then, suddenly, my oldest baby brother called and asked if he could bring his new girlfriend and her two daughters, ages five and one, to stay with us. When I asked why, he explained that she needed to get clean from methamphetamines in order to keep custody of her kids. They owed a cartel dealer a lot of money and needed a place to hide. My brother and I had always been close growing up, so I agreed. I told him to come, and they were there within a few hours.

I never imagined he would bring drugs into my house. When they arrived, they slept for what seemed like days. I was left to take care of my three kids, including the newborn, as well as her two. I was expected to handle it all on my own. A few days later, he had made some contacts with the neighbors to babysit all five kids, and we'd party when we returned. I'd never done meth before, but I thought, "Just once won't hurt." Oh, how wrong I was.

After a few months, we lost our apartment and moved into a townhouse across town, closer to their jobs. His girlfriend wasn't allowed to come downstairs except to cook for her kids, and when he was home, they were always fighting.

She would scream in agony, and at the time, I didn't understand why. Now I know she was desperately craving more meth. Soon, my brother found a dealer at his job, and my husband was using it without me. One day, my brother's girlfriend came downstairs and tried to throw hot grease on me, but instead, it hit her dog. Furious, she attacked me, punching me in the face. I took the kids and walked to my fiancé's job to tell him what had happened, then walked back to the apartment, only to be met with an enraged brother minutes later. He stormed in, came straight for me as if I had started everything, picked me up, and body-slammed me onto the floor, missing the mattress on the way down. He then ran upstairs, and I could hear him physically punishing her, literally spanking her over and over. He came back down and went to work.

Soon after, my fiancé and I moved out and found a new apartment near our first place. Things seemed quiet again. He kept working at the hardware store, and I stayed home with the kids. Then, I was offered the position of apartment manager, which I gladly accepted. But soon after, he got fired, and I was the only one working. I took on a second job as a hostess at a nearby restaurant, then a third job as a dancer on the weekends after my hostess shifts. He stayed home with the kids.

My brother came back for a visit and brought meth with him. We all went into the bathroom, smoked together, and after he left, we kept doing it every day. My fiancé refused to get a job, and I struggled to keep up with three jobs, no rest for days. He would lock me out of the house sometimes for hours, and one day, I heard my daughter screaming. I had to break the window to get in. He had her in the bathtub, doing God knows what. He claimed he was just giving her a bath, but something felt wrong, so I called the police. They arrested him for sexually assaulting both of my children.

How could I have missed it? I had always taught my daughter to tell me if anything like that was going on. How long had he been doing this? We had been together for five years. I was crushed, devastated, and consumed by guilt. My drug use only worsened from there. I moved myself and the kids into the drug dealer's house, quit both my manager and hostess jobs, and went into dancing full-time at some of the best-known strip clubs in Dallas. I was making tens of thousands of dollars a week, and all of it went straight to my dealer. He kept the money stacked in the dresser drawer, filling all three drawers on one side.

One morning, as I was showering, my dealer asked me to stick my arm out of the shower. I didn't even think, I just did as I was told. I felt a sharp sting, then blacked out. When I came to, I was naked, holding onto the bathroom door, two hours later. That's when my life as a junkie truly began.

Chapter 8

A Junkie Nightmare

I jumped from club to club, desperately trying to hide the needle marks, searching for places to shoot up where I wouldn't get caught. He became my pimp, leaving my children alone in his apartment while he guarded me from harm as I met with johns. My father had always told me growing up that this was what I would become. God wasn't even a thought in my mind as I spiraled deeper. Satan's grip on me tightened with every passing day.

The days turned into weeks, the weeks into months, and the months into a year. Time seemed to stand still, each moment blending into the next. It felt like only a month or two had passed, but I knew it had been much longer. I tried to comfort myself by telling myself I was still beautiful, but I was heartbroken. I felt so ashamed of myself.

I tried to commit suicide again, convinced that my children deserved a better life than the one I was giving them, the life of a junkie mom. Eighteen months after I started using needles, I cried out to God, begging him to take me. Death was literally at my bedside. I could feel the presence of something dark, a tall figure, coming for me. As I stood there, I begged God to either help me get clean or take me away. The overdose passed, and I finally made a decision. I was going to leave this life behind, get my children out of the mess I had created, and give them the life they deserved. One far better than what I had given them.

The next day, I called my brother and asked if I could come stay with him. At this point, I weighed only 94 pounds. He agreed, but asked me to bring him an ounce of meth. I knew my dealer had left and wouldn't be back for hours, so I quickly grabbed the kids' things and a few of my own, met with my dealer to get the drugs, and then headed to my brother's. He was four hours away, and I was terrified the dealer was following me the whole way. When I arrived, I handed over the drugs, but my brother and his girlfriend locked themselves in their room for days, refusing to share any of the dope with me.

I was lucky not to suffer withdrawals, but that was the last time I ever touched meth. I made a promise to myself and to God that I would never touch it again, and I kept that promise. God freed me from that life of bondage, and the chain was broken for good.

Soon after, I was called back to Dallas to testify against my ex for molesting my daughter. I had regretted writing that statement. I wanted my family back together. I wasn't sure if the drugs had clouded my mind and made me see things that weren't real, and I doubted everything I had said. He was acquitted of the charges, and I was arrested for outstanding traffic warrants. The children were taken into DFPS custody, and my mother came to take them.

I knew I had messed up. I had let my daughter down, just as my mother had let me down. The generational curse seemed to continue with me. My daughter didn't deserve my failure to protect her. Once I was released, I made my way to my mom's, feeling like I had failed my children, but hoping somehow, I could make things right. As of today I have 20 years sober.

Chapter 9

Getting The Snake Head

When my ex moved back to town, he set up a tent outside my mom's house. I'm sure he wasn't supposed to be there, but soon my loneliness overtook my better judgment. DFPS was no longer part of the equation, and slipping back into a relationship with him just seemed to happen. He found a job, and soon we moved in with him. He started drinking again, wetting the bed, and smoking crack, which I occasionally indulged in. I put a stop to the crack, but he kept drinking.

About eight months later, I started seeing someone else. On the day I was finally planning to leave my ex for good, DFPS took custody of my children again because I was still living with him. I tried to explain that I was leaving, but it didn't matter. My toxic decisions had led to my children being taken once more. I went through rehab, found a job, and got an apartment. Things were looking up, and I started getting visits with my kids again.

Then, I met a black man who introduced me to a whole new level of ecstasy. I became completely wrapped up in sexual pleasure, which seemed to matter more to me at the time. Deep down, though, I felt uneasy. My gut, or maybe God, kept telling me that it wasn't right, but Satan whispered otherwise. That is, until he beat me badly, and after I reported him, my children were no longer allowed to see me. We were held overnight at the police station for minor assault charges. It was the first time I had ever defended myself from abuse, and we parted ways.

I met a firefighter who took me in and helped me regain custody of my children. He also encouraged me to take classes at the Mosaic Center, where I learned skills to become an office assistant and a homemaker. I learned how to type, sew, and even some child psychology to help my kids cope with their emotions. For two years, I stayed on track, making progress. I volunteered in the rehab department at the fire station, helping at fire scenes and search and rescues, handing out water and supplies to the firefighters. I truly enjoyed this work.

Eventually, I moved into my own trailer and was finally reunited with my children. We were planning to celebrate Christmas when my step-niece, who wasn't related by blood, wanted to come stay with my daughter. They had such a great time together.

The mobile home park I moved into had my boyfriend's best friend, who was the city marshal, living there as well. I had a desire for him and ended up sleeping with him once. Soon after, I broke up with the firefighter and met the man I would spend the next ten years with. He came to pick up my niece, asked me on a date, and despite not being my usual type. He was short, had no top teeth, and dark skin. I was intrigued because he was Native American. I took his number but declined his invitation. Looking back, I wonder why I didn't choose the city marshal. I know he would have treated me well, like a princess.

In a moment of loneliness, I called my niece's father, never having learned how to respect myself. I told him he was going to "get lucky" that night. He told me he had just gotten out of prison, but I didn't care. I slept with him that night, and for some reason, I didn't want to let him go. He seemed to be the perfect match for me sexually, so I asked him to move in, which he did. He had no job, no income, but I didn't care, as long as he didn't stop having sex with me. Six months after meeting, we were married. My brother hated him because my brother had been married to his ex. After the courthouse wedding, with "I don't care what they say, I'm in love with you" playing on the radio, I felt rebellious, knowing my brother disapproved.

I withdrew all my savings to buy him tools for a job out of town. He was gone for a week, and I called him, crying, afraid I'd lose him if he kept working out of town. He came back, but soon after, I lost my job due to an overbearing boss, and we were evicted from our home. We spent three days at the lake until he secured a place with his friend. That didn't last long, though, because his friend's wife and I got into a physical fight over her pulling her toddler's hair in front of me. I lost it and attacked her. My husband then got us a room at a hotel, working for them in exchange for the room.

I think the hurricane that came through was God's warning about what was to come. My husband started a business with someone who became a great friend. Soon, the money was rolling in, and the contracts kept getting bigger and better. We moved into a house twelve miles out of town, both got trucks, and everything seemed perfect in such a short time.

Chapter 10

I Prayed For You

When we were just dating, he told me, "I prayed for someone like you." I shared my story with him, how I never wanted to feel unwanted again. He promised me he would never hurt me. Our one-year anniversary was approaching, and he planned a romantic dinner in a nearby town. I thought it was so sweet and thoughtful. But the day after our anniversary dinner, my daughter's friend came to the house and told me that my husband had been caught kissing a much younger woman who worked at a local gas station he often stopped at.

I couldn't help myself. When he called to say he would be home after stopping at Home Depot, I immediately felt something was off. He hated Home Depot; he always preferred Lowe's for supplies. My instincts screamed at me to get in the truck and go check if he was meeting her there. He had a loud stereo system in his truck, one you could hear from half a block away, so I heard him coming. I parked on the side of the store where he couldn't see me, but he didn't stop there. Instead, he turned down a road just in front of the store, where I was told she lived. I waited until I didn't hear his truck anymore, knowing he was at her house.

I drove around the block, came up the opposite way, and found him on her porch with her sitting on his lap. I threw my ring at him, told him it was over, and my daughter, who was with me, yelled, "How could you, Dad?" She was so upset. She loved me dearly and had always chosen me for him, hoping I would be the one to settle him down and keep him out of prison. I ugly-cried for days. He tried to hold me that night, but the hurt was so intense. It was the first time I had ever felt pain like that.

He knew how important marriage and my vows to God were to me. I had promised myself I would never go through another failed marriage, but I didn't know which was worse; the physical abuse I had endured in my past relationships, or the devastation of an unfaithful husband. At least the physical pain eventually faded. My trust was shattered.

After weeks of trying to gather myself, he convinced me not to leave, asking for another chance. I agreed, but insisted he get a job out of town, and we would move as far away from her as possible. He agreed, and within the year, we moved. While he was finalizing all the paperwork, he did handyman work at the mobile home park where we lived. It took some time, but he eventually got clearance for a job as a pipefitter at a refinery. Things seemed to be getting back on track, but the affair was never far from my mind. He had a routine for work every morning, and anything outside of that raised questions with me. He did everything to reassure me, until I found out he had been seeing escorts on Backpage. When I confronted him, he excused it by saying it was his buddy using his phone. I let it slide, but kept it in my mind.

A year later, I began to feel uneasy. One morning, he put on cologne, and instantly, red flags shot up. As he left and drove down the driveway, I saw him on the phone. I followed him to a nearby donut shop and saw him meeting a car with two women inside. One of them got out of the car and into his truck. She was wearing the same work attire as him. I assumed they had met at work, but when I confronted him, he denied it, even though I saw it with my own eyes. He made me feel stupid and crazy, like I hadn't seen what I had.

Then, he started taking me to strip clubs on dates. At first, I didn't mind. I even enjoyed it. A year later, we relocated to Baytown, where he transferred for work. We lived in an apartment at first, then moved into a trailer. While we were there, my daughter gave birth to a beautiful baby girl, but tragically lost her due to drugs and gang affiliation. We were asked to take custody of her, and we started raising her as our own, hoping for adoption in the near future.

We eventually moved into a house. We only had one teenager left at home, along with the baby. The electric bill was high, so we found another house with a huge yard. I started medical school, and the baby was in daycare. I finally felt important again. I did my externship at a doctor's office, waiting on my background clearance from the sheriff's office to come back. Afterward, I took a position two hours away, but the travel time became difficult, so I left that job. Then, I received approval to work at the sheriff's department. I worked there for about seven months before my daughter called to say she was pregnant, and DFPS wanted to take the baby when she was born. I went to the hospital, and sure enough, DFPS took custody of the baby. They immediately asked me to take custody, and the next day, we were in front of a judge for an emergency hearing. A day later, we had custody of another baby.

At two days old, this little girl lit up my life and changed my world forever. I had to quit my job at the sheriff's office to take care of her full-time. Meanwhile, we were still visiting swingers' clubs in downtown Houston, leaving the kids with a nanny overnight while we did things no married couple should be doing.

CHAPTER 11

The Beginning Of The End

This little angel grew like a weed, bringing so much joy into my life, just like her sister. It was beautiful to see them laughing and playing together. With DFPS no longer involved, I took a job at a pawn shop and put the girls in daycare. Soon, we could afford a housekeeper who also doubled as a babysitter when my husband and I wanted a night out. Our dates consisted of swingers' clubs and hotels with other couples. I felt left out of his cheating, so we agreed to open our relationship to the darkness, and it went on like that for about a year.

Then we met a polyamorous couple and became exclusive with them, so much so that we even got matching tattoos. She was the second wife, and her husband became my second husband. It felt beautiful for a time, but six months in, I wanted to actually sleep with him, which didn't sit well with my husband. He had been sleeping with our wife, and honestly, I didn't see the difference. So, the relationship split. Well, I split it anyway. I'm pretty sure my husband continued seeing them, but I was done.

When baby girl was about to turn eighteen months, my daughter called and said she was in jail and pregnant. When she got out, we let her live with us so she could stay clean, with the baby boy she had always wanted. She really wanted this baby, and that kept her clean for a while, but she started causing problems between my husband and me, and he left me for another woman. He moved in with her, saying I had too many kids for him. I never knew that was a problem. He stopped paying the bills and rent, leaving me with a teenage son, two children under four, and my pregnant daughter, all homeless.

I couldn't go to my mom's, so we moved into an abandoned house, where we jacked electricity to survive. I was incredibly sick for over nine months, vomiting frequently, losing weight, and unable to eat, everything I did eat came right back up. Being married to someone over ten years my bidy was in withdrawals from losing him. Little man was born, and we were still living in that abandoned house. I had never been homeless before, and I was devastated. I had to do something to get the kids under a stable roof.

We eventually ended up back at my mom's place for a while, about four months after my husband abandoned us. Then my sister told me my ex from high school was going to get in touch with me. My heart leapt into my throat, I was in disbelief. I had loved that guy so much when I was a teen. Could he possibly be looking to reconnect? Maybe he still loved me, and we could pick up the relationship again after thirty-five years. My stomach was filled with butterflies, and my chest pounded as I anticipated his call.

When I moved from Baytown and put my belongings in storage, I jokingly said a prayer, asking God to make the next guy a welder and a man of God, so I could have a stable, blossoming relationship. I thought if he was a man of God, I couldn't go wrong. Duck and I talked on the phone for a while, planning to meet soon. I was working as an assistant manager at a local Dollar Tree, and he had a job as a welder. I truly felt like God had answered my prayers, and this would be the love I had been missing all my life, the one to bring peace and restore my soul.

When we met up, he was staying at a sober living house and had just gotten out of prison.

Why I didn't see the red flags in the beginning is beyond my comprehension. I truly wanted it to be him. My intentions were completely pure, and I believed there was potential for us to become a great love story, that this would be the thing that redeemed my life.

Chapter 12

Duck Duck Goose

I should have never said my prayers out loud, because now I know that when they are spoken, Satan hears them too. Duck was indeed a welder and claimed to believe in God, or so he said. I would soon find out the second chance was just him playing children's games. He could wear a mask in public as if he really were a good person and man of God.

The day we met up again after 35 years, I leapt into his arms. He didn't look the same, but I didn't judge him for the extra pounds or balding hair, as looks didn't matter to me. I wanted a heart of gold and a love that was pure and true. I was a prize at 125 lbs and a size two; slim and beautiful. What man wouldn't want to give me the world? But I wasn't conceited. I was actually quite humble about my looks. I admired the way he looked me up and down, and without hesitation, he caught me in his arms and gave me a huge kiss.

He said, "Well, we can do one of two things. We can either go to a nice restaurant, or we can get a room and a pizza." He left it up to me. I hadn't had sex in months, so I chose the room and the pizza. Unknowingly, I was setting no boundaries for what was soon to become our relationship, a huge mistake on my part. What started as something that could have been beautiful quickly unraveled, and I held onto the hope that it could still be saved.

We stayed in touch over the phone for a month before I allowed him to meet the kids. He said he fell in love with the girls immediately. Six weeks later, we were making plans to move into an RV together. I moved first, and soon he left the sober living house and moved in with me and the girls. It was a nice place, and the girls had room to play. We'd cook meals together, and when he came home from work, I would take off his boots and wash his feet with a rag and warm water. Little did I know, I was washing the feet of my Judas.

The first time I moved out was due to a sex offender living on the property, and it just didn't sit well with me. I stayed with my cousin in Galveston for a few days, but it turned out she hated my family, blaming us for taking her from her mother, who was a drug addict and prostitute. I left and went back to the RV, but things weren't the same. The whole mood had shifted. We were drinking and partying a lot with his female cousin, who also lived on the property. She would blackout when she drank and get into violent arguments with her kids' dad. Things quickly escalated with her. I'd drink until I blacked out, only to wake up the next day filled with regret.

The second time I left him, he and his cousin went bar-hopping. He was supposed to be the designated driver, but he didn't come back until early the next morning, drunk. He knew I was against drinking and driving; he knew everything I had been through. So, I called my mom, and she came to get me and the girls. Once again, I was back living with her.

I started seeing a Texas Forestry firefighter. He had his own house, which was really nice, and I was hopeful about the relationship. But when he asked me what I brought to the table, I realized I had nothing to offer. I wasn't confident in myself; I didn't have a job or anything of value to give. When Duck called and wanted me back, it was easier to fall back into that familiarity. I began talking to Duck again when I moved into my niece's place, but soon they put me out, leaving me on the streets. I ended up moving into an abandoned house with my daughter, but she treated me horribly. So, Duck suggested I come to a women's shelter near him, and I did.

A month later, I had a job and my own RV. Duck was living in a sober living house again and didn't want to move back right away. For months, everything seemed to be going well, until one day, he took me to a birthday party with his female cousin and the father of her children. We were all drinking when his cousin did what she did best. Start a fight. I went inside to get her youngest out of the mix. As I headed down the stairs, I felt a shove behind me and saw her stomp on my ankle, shattering it. I blacked out from the pain.

When I came to, Duck was telling me to get up and walk to the car. I told him my ankle was broken and I couldn't walk. He just snapped, "No, it's not, walk, you dumb b%$#@," and forced me to walk unassisted. I could hear the bones crunching in my leg as I struggled to move. The dad had called the police, so we loaded up, and Duck's cousin got in the back with her kids. As the police arrived, we pulled away, and she started yelling at Duck. I asked her to lay off him and sit back, but she came over the seat, grabbed my hair with both hands, and headbutted me in the face, knocking me out. When I came to, she did it again. Duck didn't pull over or try to stop her in any way. She headbutted me another six times, pulling my hair out on both sides during the fifteen minutes it took to get to my RV.

He dropped me off in my yard, telling me to get myself inside, and then went on partying with his cousin. He said he stayed the night at his job and went to work the next day. He didn't take me for X-rays until 6 PM the following day. My ankle needed surgery, it was compared to a skydiving injury, split into three parts. He had to move in with me while I recovered, as the surgery would take ten more days. He cooked and got the kids to school, but still expected sex during my excruciating pain. It was like he had no sympathy for me at all.

During the ten weeks it took for me to recover, paying the bills became a problem for him. He threw it in my face that he was paying the bills now, making me feel obligated to have sex and start cooking meals again. He began talking to me as if I were trash, and I didn't deserve anything he did for me. It got worse if I asked him about the way he was treating me. Then, I was forced to get up, cook, and clean, even when I was in pain. Somehow, my being injured interfered with my ability to serve and do for him.

I never drank again after that. I felt like I deserved all the mistreatment, even though I had done nothing wrong.

Chapter 13

The Cycles Begin

The first three years were tough, but nothing could have prepared me for the final four years. The emotional, mental, and verbal abuse intensified, becoming worse and worse with each passing day. He started wearing a mask, treating me terribly at home while being charming around other people. After a year of constant harassment, I had had enough. I packed up and moved into a different RV, leaving him behind.

Soon, he started showing up at my door, asking for coffee, love bombing me, and promising to be better, to stop treating me like crap. He worked his way back into my heart, and I allowed him back in. Then, one night, I woke up to feel his hands on my head, my neck turned to face the door behind me. I sat up, trying to peel his hands off me, slapping at his arms. He was looking directly into my eyes when he snapped my neck. Once I heard the disc snap, he let go. I asked him what he was doing, and he told me he was trying to kiss me, that he was dreaming.

But the look in his eyes when he did that… they were black as coal, pure black with no white showing, like he was possessed by something otherworldly. I had never seen anything like that before. I laid back down as if nothing had happened, maybe in denial about the whole situation. The next day, I went back to work.

I worked for another year, and then we made plans to move into a larger place, too far for me to walk to work. He told me I didn't have to work anymore because it was his job to pay the bills and take care of things. All I had to do was take care of him and the girls. I should have known better, but I loved him so much. I believed he could be better, that he would do better. But it wasn't even a week before the cycle started all over again.

We started going to church, thinking it might improve the relationship. But all it did was give him a new mask, and he used my devotion to the Lord against me. He suggested we start couples counseling and asked me to marry him. I thought he actually meant it. We began speaking to the assistant pastor at the church and started preparing for our wedding. He helped with none of the preparations, though.

I moved into the new place, and he came about three months later. Things seemed to be going well, and we were married. But after that, he started trying to take over the discipline of the girls. I had to put a stop to it. They became so disrespectful to him, and he became a monster. I had to intervene and stop him from hitting them for absolutely no reason. He started staying in his room after we got married, yelling at us from there, barking orders, insisting on being served hand and foot because he worked. Everything was left to me, despite the fact that I had a snapped neck. I could hardly move and couldn't feel my hand anymore, but I tried my best. My lower back and hips were in severe pain as well.

I soon learned that I would need neck surgery to replace the two discs he had torn out when he snapped my neck. I would be down for another ten weeks. Then, one Sunday, the pastor of the church we were attending delivered a message that touched my soul. It was about the love of God for mankind and the love from mankind to God, an unconditional love fueled by the Spirit of God living and working inside you. I wanted that love more than anything I had ever wanted in my life. I felt the Holy Spirit inside me, growing stronger every day.

Chapter 14

Setting My Wrongs Right

Duck's efforts to destroy my sense of self-worth grew more apparent after we were married. He took out a life insurance policy on me and ramped up the gaslighting and verbal abuse. Going to church became my reprieve, my escape from his constant torment. I started asking God to fix what was broken inside me, believing that if I could change and become more obedient to His word, He would change Duck's heart and ways. For some reason, the commandments kept coming to mind during my prayers. I realized God was trying to show me there was something I wasn't in compliance with, but I was ready and willing to surrender everything to Him. I had so much unforgiveness in my heart, but I knew I had to face my demons, no matter how hard it would be.I felt if I got right with God the pain and anguish would possibly end. So I started to heal me.

The journey wasn't easy, but I pushed myself. The first person I had to forgive was my mother, because I had to honor my mother as the commandment said. I cried for weeks, recalling all the emotional baggage I had carried from her lack of protection. Over time, I started to see things from her perspective. She had been essentially a single, married woman, raising three kids on her own, working tirelessly to provide while caring for an alcoholic husband who constantly cheated on her and was in and out of jail and rehab. She had done the best she could with the circumstances she was given. Life hadn't been easy on her either. My heart forgave her, and the peace I felt made it easier to move on to the next.

I forgave my first husband, the one who had beaten me so badly. I forgave my second husband, the one who took my daughter's innocence. I forgave my third husband, the one who couldn't stop cheating. Then, I realized I had to forgive my dad too, and that realization choked me. My heart had been holding onto so much unforgiveness for the man who had stolen my innocence. But then, it happened… something divine. The Holy Spirit began working in me, healing me. I realized that the enemy no longer had a hold on my life. My heart, mind, and soul instantly felt a peace that surpassed all human understanding.

I wrote these words: "If I could take only one person to heaven, it would be the little boy my dad was, unloved, forgotten, alone, and insecure. I would hold his hand and love him so he would be understood. I would give him the love he never found, on the streets of gold and the grass all around." I wrote, "I love you, Daddy, no matter the pain. You are forgiven, and Satan is slain." Then I forgave myself for the decisions I had made.

The next person on my list, and undoubtedly the hardest, was my fourth husband. I was still in the fight for my sanity with him. How do you forgive someone you're still In a relationship with?

Chapter 15

Holy Spirit Come

My medical issues were getting worse, and I had to start using a walker because the pain in my right hip had me falling and struggling to do even the simplest everyday activities. The pain became so unbearable that I found myself contemplating suicide again. I started looking for family members who could take the girls, just so I could get a break. I had no help from my husband, and I knew I wasn't going to get any from him. He hadn't helped with my broken ankle or my neck surgery, and I was overwhelmed, desperate for it all to end, especially the mental torment he was putting me through.

I had to stop going to church because the physical pain was so unbearable, and the doctors wouldn't prescribe anything to relieve my anguish. Despite all of this, my husband still expected me to cook his meals, put up with his abuse, and take care of the girls. One day, while shopping for the girls' shoes for school, I fell from my walker and broke my elbow. He didn't even bother to help me. Instead, he stood there watching me scream, with a slight smile on his face. A stranger had to help me back into my walker, and my husband casually said, "Your arm isn't broke, get up." When I told him it was, he replied, "Well, I guess they don't get shoes then."

So, I held my arm, and my oldest girl pushed me through the store to get the shoes. It was at that moment I truly realized he was a complete sociopath. I was put in a cast and then taken home to continue my wifely duties as usual. He showed no sympathy, no empathy for me. When I couldn't do something, the girls were made to do it because he refused to clean up after them. He hated me even more because he had to cook when he came home from work.

Finally, I packed my bags, took the kids, and went to a shelter in Houston, where I stayed for a few days. But, in the end, I went right back to him.

God seemed to have more in store for me in that moment. I applied for disability, hoping to eventually have an income. He continued to give me so much grief, laying it on thick. At one point, he called me trash, and in response, I picked up the trash can and said, "This is trash, I'm not trash." He hit the can, causing it to spill all over me and the floor. I left everything behind and took the girls for a drive, hoping to calm down as he had my emotions running high.

As I drove, I started praying and crying so hard that I had to stop in the middle of the road. I screamed at God, "WHY, GOD, WHY?" I pounded my fist on the steering wheel, shouting, "God, why me? No more, please, God!" The song on the radio, Perfectly Loved by Rachel Lampa, began playing, and in that moment, the Holy Spirit came to me, wrapping me in its embrace. I could physically feel the Lord take me in His arms, wiping my tears, telling me how perfectly loved I truly was, and reminding me that I didn't need anything more than what God had for me. Right there in the middle of the road that day, I found the agape love I had longed for.

I vowed to accept that love and give it in return. That's all I would ever need or want again. I accepted the Savior for the second time that day. Suddenly, I was awakened to what God wanted for me. I had clarity and discernment about what I needed to do and how to react to my abuser.

My mentor at the church kept encouraging me to stay loyal to my husband as he continued to abuse me. She would dismiss my complaints, calling him a "thorn in my side." I eventually gave up on her advice because I knew I deserved so much more. My prayers became different; more precise, as the Bible says, "Ask and you shall receive." Nothing was too big for God. When I returned home, his rants and words no longer hurt. I stopped reacting to his triggering words. I did what was required, no more, no less. I began focusing on healing, working on myself from the inside out. He couldn't take that from me.

I began to forgive him and understand that he was projecting his own insecurities onto me, stemming from a broken childhood of his own. I knew he was never going to change… for me, at least. Maybe one day, for God, but that was between him and God. I couldn't hold myself to the potential I once saw in him. Slowly, things began to improve, and I felt free.

The Lord gave me a rapture dream. I dreamed of fire falling from the sky to earth, zombie-like beings holding guns, and snakes slithering on the ground. I could feel the Lord calling His children home. The dreams and visions became more frequent and profound, awakening my soul to His words. I became increasingly obedient to what He needed from me.

I had to move in with a friend due to the overwhelming roach problem in our place. He refused to clean, and the girls were too little to keep up. My friend quickly had her sister kick me out after I gave Duck grace and let him move in with me. So, we had to find another place.

When we moved back into our own place, it wasn't even a month before it all started again. I knew it was only a matter of time, but I had faith that the Lord would deliver me from this torment. I knew I was His child, and Jesus would bring me close, showing me a vision of angels in the clouds, holding the Lamb's Book of Life. I saw Him wearing the crown of thorns atop His head on the cross, and I knew I was with Him in that moment. On His mind, in His heart. He thought of everyone and loved us so much as he hung on the cross. I continued to pray and thank Him for the excruciating pain in my hip, knowing that, through it all, He was with me.

Eventually, I had my hip replaced, but Duck only helped me for three days. I eventually found a provider to come in and assist, but everything remained the same with him, except I had changed. My mindset was completely different now. Once I recovered, the pain subsided, and I had already healed from the emotional scars of his abuse. God told me, "It’s time now."

It would take months for my disability to come through, but during that time, my relationship with the Lord grew stronger each day. My only grandson was taken from my daughter, and we began the home study to have him placed with his sisters and me. However, DFPS didn’t approve of his background because Duck was a four-time convicted felon. Despite the setbacks, I continued to visit him nearly every weekend. It was during this time that I began hearing the angels singing after my prayers each night, and I knew that God was calling me to move out and pursue custody of my grandson. And so, I did just that. I applied for public housing and sought legal aid for a divorce.

My prayers became filled with praise and thanksgiving for delivering me to a place of peace. I prayed for my enemies to receive blessings, and most importantly, I invited the Holy Spirit into the raising of my grandchildren, asking the Lord to receive glory from their lives. Psalm 40 says, “I waited patiently for the Lord; He turned to me and heard my cry. He lifted me out of the slimy pit, out of the mud and mire. He set my feet upon a rock, giving me a firm place to stand. He put a new song in my mouth, a hymn of praise to our God. Many will see and fear and put their trust in Him.” Amen.

I want to say thank you to my Lord and Savior for trusting me with the responsibility of raising this beautiful family in the way they should go. With all the beautiful Christian music out there, all I have to do every morning is turn on my playlist and come into His presence, transporting myself right into the arms of the Father. I know He lingers with me daily. He is waiting for each of you, longing to hold you just as He holds me. I pray to seek his face in everything I do.

With all the trauma I've endured in my life, seemingly more than the average person, I've been delivered and placed in peace like never before. I encourage you to place your faith in God, believing that no matter what the enemy plans, God has already won the war.

Psalm 46:10

"Be still and know that I am God; I will be exalted among the nations, I will be exalted in the earth."

Made in the USA
Coppell, TX
18 January 2026

68258951R00026